# SPIRIT

## With A Smile

The world according to BOB.

# Gregg Sanderson

Published and distributed by Transformation Publishing:
www.transformation-publishing.com

ISBN: 978-1-60166-034-3

Library of Congress:  2012934197

*Transformation* PUBLISHING

# ACKNOWLEDGMENTS

My gratitude to those who read through this book and offered their constructive suggestions and encouragement.

Paige Manuel, Edrea Kaiser, Sharon Weir, Ellin Dize, John Nestor, Carl Babcock, Natalie Amsden,
and
Marla Sanderson

# DEDICATION

This book is dedicated to those whose work had the greatest influence on my life—and never knew it:

Dr. Timothy Leary
Steve Jobs
Ken Keyes, Jr.
Ernest Holmes
And to my fellow traveler on this strange journey,
Rev. Marla Sanderson

# Praise for *Spirit with a Smile*

*"No doubt,* Spirit With a Smile *will indeed make you smile. Perhaps more important it hooks our attention in a very unassuming way inviting us to go down the rabbit hole of our own belief system where anything is possible, including a deepened sense of purpose for being on the planet. Gregg Sanderson has a gift and that gift is his ability to gently guide us back to the place we never really left--our oneness with God. With his humor and profound sense of the sacred Gregg brings us back to the remembrance of who we really are and that what we do with who we are truly matters. Read this book and may the BOB be with you!"*

— Dennis Merritt Jones, Author of *The Art of Uncertainty ~ How to Live in the Mystery of Life and Love It,* and, *The Art of Being ~ 101 Ways to Practice Purpose in Your Life*

*"If you enjoy your spirituality in a straight up, funny and sardonic way - you'll totally enjoy* Spirit with a Smile. *Gregg Sanderson shares jewels and tidbits that are so obvious when he says them that you can't believe you didn't think of them yourself! Spirituality does not have to be complicated; you don't need a guru or intermediary - all your need is common sense and a desire to be happy. If you are ready to give up your B.S. (your belief systems) then this book is for you!"*

— Sheri Rosenthal DPM author of *The Complete Idiot's Guide to Toltec Wisdom* and *Banish Mind Spam!*

"Sprit with a Smile *is an all encompassing day trip that takes us from our divine creation to the POWER of NOW! Gregg uses hummer, quantum physics and logic to unfold the simple truth that thoughts become things and our only mission on earth is to ENJOY our Life... Life is full of consequences but there are NO Coincidences.*"
— Carl Babcock: LOA Coach, Self-Proclaimed Prophet

"Spirit With A Smile *is a book to be savored morning and night because it creates the frame of mind you want to be in. From the first few pages, I knew this book was smart, funny, and helpful. Because it's written in such an enjoyable, conversational tone, it would be easy to read it quickly, and yet the ideas are deep and powerful. I'm reading it slowly so I can ponder, absorb, and remember all the good I'm getting from Gregg Sanderson's writing.*"
— Jana Stanfield, the "Queen of Heavy Mental"

"*I took the time to read this book and I loved it. I sincerely appreciate the way it brings common ideas and gentle humour to drive home such a profound idea that, when embraced, will truly change our lives. It left impressions that will easily stick with me as reminders to pay attention and take control when I find myself slipping into the abyss of my human conditions. Few books today are capable of adding valuable insights without reams of filler. This is one such book that delivers its point without wasting its readers valuable time.*"
— Dale Jukes, Spiritual Director, Okanagan Centre for Spiritual Living, Vernon BC

# Contents

# INTRODUCTION to B.S.

There are wonderful books written on the subject of Spirituality, and each reaches its appropriate audience. A great teacher once told me, "The Truth doesn't care how it's packaged," and I can say that I've gained value from every single package of Truth I've unwrapped.

Yet despite all the evidence, there's still a little voice in the back of my mind somewhere that whispers, "Aw c'mon. You don't really believe this stuff, do you?"

This book is for all who, with ten minutes or ten decades of experience with Spiritual teaching, still have that little glimmer of doubt.

This is not the "be all and end all"; it's more like the "be some and end some." There are those who have difficulty picturing the infinite (like me), so I've done what I could to describe it in a way our tiny minds might grasp. By the time you finish you may not know all there is to know about the infinite, but I'll bet you get better parking spaces.

Sometimes different words and a different point of view can create a "Wow!" that's been waiting to burst out. Perspective stimulates understanding, and often a different viewpoint can be the perfect bridge to applied

Spirituality.

This is another way of looking at "The Way Things Are" that could prove useful. When I state (and I will) my theory of the purpose of life, it is not a position I'll defend to the death – but it'll sure make living more fun. I also think it's worthwhile to look at life with a little more humor, so here we'll approach life with a chuckle.

## Belief Systems

"A belief system is just a thought you keep thinking," says Abraham-Hicks. From militant Atheism to the strictest Fundamentalism; from radical vegan to raving carnivore; from Socialist to Libertarian, we are run by our belief systems. They influence everything from sex, religion, and politics to life itself, before, during, and after.

With all the conflicting belief systems in the world, how can we tell which ones work? Here's the big secret. They all do.

Indeed, every belief creates its corresponding circumstance. The more restrictive our beliefs, the more restrictive are our lives. For purpose of instructive abbreviation, I will use the initials of Belief System throughout.

If my B.S. says, "Life is difficult," I struggle without satisfaction.

If my B.S. says, "I'm a guilty sinner," I live in wretched¬ness and remorse.

If my B.S. says, "Poverty is a virtue," I envy the successful.

If my B.S. says, "There's not enough," I never stop looking for more.

If my B.S. says, "It's cold and flu season," I know just when to sneeze.

If my B.S. says, "I'm born to suffer," my happiness comes with guilt.

If my B.S. says, "I'll never love again," I create my own loneliness.

If my B.S. says, "I'm not worthy," I live life as a loser.

Are you getting the instructive part of the abbreviation? Suppose instead:

My B.S. says, "Life is easy," I might not kill myself working.

My B.S. says, "Not Guilty," I could live in innocence.

My B.S. says, "It's good to be rich," it would be OK to make lots of money.

My B.S. says, "Life is abundant," I'd reap the bounty.

My B.S. says, "Joy is my birthright," I wouldn't need misery.

My B.S. says, "Perfect health is natural," I'd swallow fewer pills.

My B.S. says, "Love is all around," I'd live in ecstasy.

My B.S. says, "I deserve the best," I'd enjoy it more.

Some B.S.es are better than others, but they're still B.S.

You may argue this point. You may say, "I believe in prosperity, but I'm still broke." Or, "I went to a relationship seminar, but I'm still a jerk." Or, "I eat the right foods and do healthy stuff, but I'm still sick."

If you want a clue as to why such beliefs aren't working, remember the quote at the beginning of this section: "A belief system is just a thought you keep thinking." Each of the first group of statements gets negated before it's even spoken. Five minutes of affirmation might not be enough to counter 23 hours and 55 minutes of the opposite belief.

What I offer here is more B.S. — another way to picture life and the Universe that makes sense or not, depending upon your B.S. If your B.S. is B.S., what have you got to lose by living with THIS B.S.? It's all B.S. anyhow, so you might as well have fun with it.

Yet it doesn't take any B.S. to scratch my nose. It itches, I scratch. That's how it works. That's how the Universe works, too ... no matter what your B.S.

# 1 THE WAY IT IS
## (Unless It's Something Else)

*"The world is ready for a mystic revolution..."*
*— George Harrison*

In the Introduction we talked about Belief Systems (B.S.) and how they work. The rest of this book will present a new belief system that isn't really new, but is couched in language that might provoke an "Aha" or two, or maybe even an "Oi Vey!"

In our material world, stuff is three-dimensional. Everything has length, width, and depth. Think for a moment and you'll realize there are additional dimensions that make up our reality. Two that occur offhand are Space and Time. Anything that has length, width, and depth must also occupy space and time.

Streetttttchhh your mind and consider there may be other dimensions as well. We have emotions which help define our reality here. We also have intelligence which allows us rationality. Could these be additional dimensions?

Suppose they extend through other dimensions as yet inconceivable to us? It's reasonable to assume rocks don't have emotions, and animals have emotions but not intelligence. Can we figure that these two dimensions, while present in our world, could also span into other dimensions? Sure. Maybe we can consider creative power a dimension, or perhaps Life itself. Why not?

Although our concern now is with the five dimensions of our physical world, the others are also present, and we can only imagine their extent. Now, before the elastic in our stretched minds snaps us back to limitation, let's exercise the imagination.

## The World According to BOB

Imagine a strange Entity.

It has no personality; in fact It isn't a person.

It is neither solid, liquid, nor gas and exists in dimensions beyond our ken.

Imagine It in a room about the size of your living room, and to nourish the imagination, we'll use new dimensions to describe It. Instead of solid, liquid and gas, or length, width, and depth, let them be thought, feeling, and stuff, the world of all the other dimensions we talked about.

This Entity is raw power. It has the ability to do anything … anything at all or nothing at all. The power in the leg of a gnat, and the power of a million suns is all the same and all a part of our Entity. Think electricity on steroids.

Feeling: Feeling is the Motive Force behind the power. This dimension of our Entity impels and propels it like voltage to the electric current. In the beginning, the only emotion is bliss — Love without an object.

**Thought:** There is thought that directs the power to its ultimate activity. It decides where to apply power and feelings propel it to its destination where it does what it is directed to do.

**Stuff:** Finally is the substance — the stuff — energy in motion, vibrating like crazy. It's what the thought and feeling act upon. Imagine our Entity, a self-contained sculptor, with sheer brilliance guiding the feelings to sculpt the stuff.

Now picture this multi-dimensional Entity, feeling, energy, and stuff all contained within it, filling up the whole room.

Take a minute to catch your breath and get a picture of this Being in that room.

It isn't doing anything. It's just being there. It's "being", not "doing". Its only feeling is bliss. Since It's all that fills the room, there's nothing outside of Itself to fear, get angry at, or worry about. There's not even anything to love outside of Itself. Bliss is all there is — raw love without an object.

To help our limited imaginations, let's take this Whatever-It-Is and create It in our image (it's been done before). It's a Being of Bliss, so we'll call It by the acronym BOB for short. But remember, it's not really a person.

BOB was Thought, Feeling and Stuff all at once, and blissfully hanging out. It knew all there was to know, which was nothing. It had the power to do anything it wanted, but there was nothing to do, and all was bliss because there were no other emotions.

"In the beginning was the Word ..." but BOB didn't know any words and didn't have anything to say anyhow, because nothing was happening. REALLY nothing. Zip! Zero! Nada! It was just hanging out in Its little room.

It was Brilliance with nothing to think about; Omnipotence with nothing to control; Love without an object; and Stuff without form.

Then, on the first of Forever, BOB awoke to an idea. As we know, energy can't be created or destroyed. It can only change form as it vibrates slower or faster. BOB thought, "Hey, I can slow down parts of my own stuff and make things out of Me."

So Thought sent a message through Love to some of the Stuff "SLOW DOWN." It did, and then there was matter. What a BOB!

BOB filled Its room with little stars and planets, and all sorts of groovy things made out of Itself. Since everything was still a part of BOB, but slowed down a little, It got to experience being a planet, a star, and even a rock. All that stuff was pretty, but it was only stuff, and let's face it, a rock doesn't have a very exciting life. Put lots of rocks together and they're still just rocks. After a while BOB got tired of making rocks in Its room.

So, BOB incorporated another dimension to Its entertainment. It added Feeling, and made things out of Its stuff that also could feel. If It had created vocabulary It would have called the things "bugs" or "fish" or "animals" or "dinosaurs". They were all made out of BOB stuff but had the extra advantage of feeling. They acted on instinct but provided generations of entertainment for our BOB… But it was out of balance. BOB needed to add thought, the next step — the dimension of mind. Then they'd be just like BOB, only different.

This was the tricky part, because BOB's mind created all the things, and planets, and animals, and bugs, and such. What would happen if It created other beings that could also think? They would have to be able to think of anything at all, and Thought directing feeling creates stuff. BOB couldn't limit what they'd think, because it wouldn't be "thinking" any more.

BOB took a chance.

It added thought and made people, and since they were made out of BOB, they were also part of the Thought, Feeling, and Stuff and had all the power of BOB. Their mind was BOB's Mind. Love was the only emotion, and they could mold and direct BOB's power to create whatever they wanted. All they had to do was think about it and love it.

The same way we can watch a couple of TV shows at once, BOB lived many human lives at the same time. It experienced a wide variety of new things through them and loved every minute of it. The people had a proclivity to create for themselves.

Just as our human brain directs parts of our body, so it was with BOB. When a part of our body is out of line, our nervous system tells us about it and we do what we can to ease the pain, scratch the itch, or enhance the pleasure. BOB does the same.

A person BOB made out of Its stuff has a situation, and BOB immediately sets out to rectify or magnify it. How does It know? Because the person thinks about it, and the thoughts are directly connected to BOB's mind with the force of the Love. Remember, it's all BOB in that room.

BOB figures "If they think it, they want it." and proceeds to deliver it in a way that will lead toward the most happiness BOB could enjoy through them.

The only rule for each person was "We become what we believe."

Since it was all BOB, the people learned the rule right away and had a dandy time creating anything they wanted as easily as a smile. They'd think a thought; it would happen; and BOB enjoyed the show. It got to experience this thing It called "Life" through each one of Its creations and all of them at once.

Everything was part of BOB, so there was no way anybody could be harmed. The "love it" part was especially easy, since there were no other emotions. All people had to do was put their attention on what they wanted to be, do, or have. The message would travel to the Master Intelligence propelled by Love. It would then fill the request by adjusting the stuff of BOB to satisfy the want.

BOB loved to create and every time a thought came, It got to share the joy of the receiver. It was a win at both ends of the deal, and BOB got very good at bringing forth anything that would produce more love and joy.

Think of it as BOB.com, the Supreme Superstore. Place your order via e (emotion)-mail. BOB.com makes and ships it and It's never out of stock. BOB.com's motto is "You ask for it. You got it."

If a person wanted a house, and another was a builder, BOB knew that instantly and put them together. One person sneezes, another shows up with an extra handkerchief. Nothin' to it. "Believe it and it's done."

BOB was happy and loved Its people. What's not to love? Each was a part of BOB and It got to enjoy life in a myriad of different ways through the love of all the different people It created.

Everything was blissful and lovey dovey. Soon (in BOB time, actually gazillions of years) lovey dovey became samey samey and BOB decided to make it more interesting.

## The Game

The Force we know as BOB couldn't change Its

nature, but It could make it a game and not tell the people their thought could create. BOB could play Its game and enjoy the new thrill of discovery. With a cosmic chuckle, BOB called Its new game "Hide and Find."

Ooops! Now the people had to make their own rules, and they made a couple of "Rules for Living" that complicated the game. But, no matter what happened, it provided BOB with entertaining consequences.

BOB, as is Its nature, would manifest everybody's thoughts in the best possible way. Although BOB preferred the happy endings, It enjoyed the complex plot lines, dramas, and adventures people created for themselves as all sought happiness according to their beliefs.

Without realizing it, they added extra obstacles to the game and played it with two innocent sounding rules that don't work. We call them the RACE Trap rules. Some would figure them out and be happy. Some wouldn't and would spend their lives trying to work the unworkable.

## The RACE Trap Rules

### Rule 1. Righteousness.

*You must always be right. You must think the right thoughts, feel the right feelings, have the right friends, belong to the right club, say and do the right thing…and on and on, always RIGHT.*

This is a good one. BOB has all sorts of adventures with it. Why, people even use it as an excuse to go to war. That's entertaining, and nothing is really lost, since it's all BOB stuff anyhow.

Judgment of "right" and "wrong" separates people into "Us"s and "Them"s in a whole bunch of different ways. Like blind men touching different parts of the elephant, each has his own "right" view of BOB. That's funny, because they each think BOB is on their side, and they're all right because everything is BOB.

People separate themselves by color, geography, sex, age, tribe... even beliefs! Through them BOB experiences all sorts of new things: fear, anger, hatred, jealousy, justification, embarrassment, guilt, condemnation, forgiveness, conquest, valor, glory! That one little rule would keep BOB entertained for a long time. And the Love would be underneath it all the time, although not all would discover it.

The only difference between an Albert Schweitzer and an Osama bin Laden is the product of each one's beliefs, and BOB experiences life accordingly through each. If the B.S. generates love, the creative energy mingles with other energy from those of like mind to advance, as best as possible, toward a Happy Ending. If the B.S. generates hatred, the creative energy mingles with other energy from those of like mind to advance, as best as possible, toward a Happy Ending. It might be a longer journey, but it all goes into the creative mix in the direction of a Happy Ending.

### Rule 2. Approval.

*Anybody who isn't you is automatically better than you, and it's your job to please them and gain their approval.*

This adds another dimension to the game. With this, not only must people always be right, they have to convince others of their righteousness and gain their approval. What fun!

Now we have people seeking approval from people, who are seeking approval from people, who are seeking approval from people, who are seeking approval from people, who are seeking approval ... Well, you get the idea.

Mix it with Righteousness and BOB gets to add to Its experience such delights as anxiety, humiliation, authority, supplication, politics, slavery, prestige, judgment, embarrassment, individuality, status, not to mention feelings of inferiority and superiority. Now the game is REALLY interesting, thanks to the RACE Trap rules.

RACE is an acronym, and another instructive abbreviation. It stands for "**R**ighteousness and **A**pproval **C**omplicate **E**verything," and when thoughts are influenced by them we call it the "RACE Trap."

## Expansion

Love and creative power are still underneath it all, since BOB is all there is in that room, and the cardinal rule is the same, "Thought is creative." But now RACE Trap rules confuse the issue because the people spend more time thinking about what they DON'T want, so they get more of that. The Creative Power BOB still says, "Yes" no matter what folks are thinking about. It has to.

Now here comes another stretch. Expand the walls, floor, and ceiling of the room outward to Infinity. Everything is still the same. All the people are intelligent and creative and made of the same BOB stuff, which now fills all the space. Even you and me.

Get it? We're US and all part of BOB.

WOW!

Finally, drop the anthropomorphic comparison and once again realize that BOB is RESPONSIVE INTEL¬LIGENCE, AND CREATIVE POWER THAT WORKS WITH ENERGY THROUGH EMOTIONS. The Being Of Bliss now fills all space and time and other dimensions we can't even imagine.

BOB isn't a person (Can I say that often enough?), It's a Power and we're all connected to It through our minds and feelings. We're all made from the stuff of BOB and It experiences our lives through each of us.

The game is to "get it" that our thoughts create our world, otherwise we will need to come back again and again until we do. No matter what we do, it's all BOB acting through us. The more we get it, the more good feelings we send to BOB, and the more we enjoy our lives (and the more BOB enjoys us, too).

The truth is still the same as when BOB was in the little room:

The RACE Trap rules don't work.

Thought is creative.

Our emotions communicate our thoughts.

BOB responds and always says, "Yes."

And that's the way it is (unless it's something else).

# 2 HOW IT WORKS

*"Imagination is the beginning of creation."*
*– George Bernard Shaw*

Now that we've learned thought is creative, I guess it's reasonable to ask "How does it create?" Many of us, I'm sure, can say we've thought many thoughts that haven't created a darn thing (or so we've thought). One of those thoughts might be that it hasn't created anything, so that thought also came about.

Frustrating, isn't it. And with the energy of frustration, It continues to create nothing because frustration is the propelling force behind the thought. As long as we think nothing happens, nothing happens. Put a little emotion behind it and nothing REALLY happens.

BOB is everywhere, and we're all part of that BOB. Our human minds have a direct wire to BOB Mind, and since BOB Mind is in contact with every human mind, It's able to answer the mental request by arranging the affairs, stage and actors in the best possible way to enrich the symphony we call life.

## The Role of Emotion

Here's how to differentiate between idle musings and the thoughts that create all the various realities. The creative thoughts have the force of emotion behind them. The others get lost in the shuffle.

That can be a plus or a minus, depending upon the feeling. The stronger and more pleasant the emotion, the more satisfying will be the resulting situation. Feelings brought about through a distorted belief system could create thoughts that produce a much less pleasing outcome.

Suppose, for example, a relationship breaks up and you think they "...done you wrong." You feel resentful, hurt, angry, and beneath all that is the fear that you screwed up, or that you'll never find another, or you're a mess, or any of many other disasters that may befall you because of it.

In the throes of that, you may tell yourself a variety of unhelpful things, such as "Men (women) are no damn good.", "I'll never let anybody hurt me like that again.", "I can't keep a relationship.", "Nobody loves me", "I can't do anything right" — and on and on. Declare all this with strong emotions behind it, and your next relationship could be a real doozy.

Your feelings set the creative declarations in motion. That's why it's called "emotion".

## Intelligence

This is the other essential part of the creative process. If emotion is the force behind the power of the creative process, Thinking sets the direction. Since your human intelligence is irreversibly connected to the Mind of BOB there's never (underline NEVER) any separation, so what you think is what you get (where have we heard that before?).

It's all the same BOB stuff, so when the human mind thinks it, BOB Mind gets it right away and sets about the business of creating. The problem comes in when we try to tell BOB how to do it. You see, BOB has a vantage point where It's aware of Its whole infinitude, so It can arrange all the pieces in a much better way than we can.

What we do with our little minds is try to figure out just how BOB will give us what we ask for. Within the boundaries of our limited perception we don't have a lot to work with. It's as if we were trying to travel with a road map that only had one road on it, while BOB uses the satellite view. The more we dwell on "how" the more it confuses or delays the answer to our request.

Our job is to know where we're going, and then turn it over to BOB to get us there. In a nutshell, it's "I know what, BOB knows how."

You may ask, "If that's the way it works, how come the world is in such a mess?" The answer is, because of the RACE Trap rules — **R**ighteousness and **A**pproval **C**omplicate **E**verything. That's the game, and a lot of people aren't playing it very well.

## It shall be done according to your B.S.

It all comes down to Belief Systems (B.S.). If you believe being right is very important, your thinking might be distorted by resentment, anger, revenge, hostility, fear, or other emotions foreign to the true nature of BOB. It can lead you to create situations and people in your life that will challenge your assumptions, actions, and beliefs.

If you believe your happiness somehow depends upon the reaction of some other individual, group, or impersonal "others," then your thinking could be colored by guilt, fear, frustration, embarrassment, humiliation, and other worries. With that qualification, you can attract a supply of critics and disapproval into your world that will keep you in line until you learn there is no line.

There are almost infinite combinations of righteousness and approval, and BOB will always create exactly what gets your attention. Thought is creative, and that's how it has to work. It's all BOB can do because you're a part of It and It has so much love for you (Itself) that It can't do anything less.

So, what we need to do is somehow get past the RACE Trap, and create a new belief that works for us instead of against us.

It's easy. The tough part is giving up the stuff that doesn't work because we get it thrown at us daily and usually just swallow it without a second thought. Imagine all the influences around us that want us to do the "right" thing, eat the "right" food, live in the "right" part of town, vote for the "right" candidate, go to the "right" schools, choose the "right" career, and of course find Mr. or Ms. "Right".

We know if we use the "right" deodorant, we won't offend "others" and we can always get admiration and status if we drive the "right" car and dress to impress. Then there are the myriad of items advertised to make us popular, admired, and most likely anxious that somebody might not like us. You may not believe this, but some people even form their opinions based upon what their peers think. Imagine that.

Parents give us examples, churches give us orders, fairy tales give us models, schools give us misinformation, songs give us reactions… and on and on. Is it any wonder that what we create isn't always what we think we want?

What do we really want? Of course, since we're made out of BOB stuff, we want what BOB wants.

And what does BOB want? Read on.

# 3 BOB JUST WANTS TO HAVE FUN

*"Joy delights in Joy"*
*— William Shakespeare*

By now you may have figured out that the story of Intelligence and Power we call BOB has some parallels with the mythology in various holy books. The tree of knowledge for example, could have something to do with righteousness since the knowledge is of good and evil, right and wrong. The story of Cain and Abel vying for their daddy's favor might have something to do with approval. Ya think?

Since every thought is a request, BOB gets a lot of conflicting requests. If you ask for something you don't want, BOB gives you what you ask for. Have you ever said; "I'm fat," then wonder why you have trouble losing weight? You just spoke your word for FAT. BOB isn't a mind reader, you know. Oh wait! Yes It is.

Emotions are the energy to communicate with BOB, and they're often beneath the surface, so if you say "I feel good" when you feel lousy, BOB will not be fooled. You'll get more "lousy." Then there's preponderance. If you spend a half-hour a day "thinking positive" and the rest of the time living and thinking negative, what do you figure BOB will create for you?

I know some people who, when invited to go for coffee after their prosperity class, said, "I can't afford it." Hmmm.

So what's a body to do? Simple. Just be clear, happy, and creative 24/7… and apply for sainthood. As for the rest of us, let's just do what we can when we can with what we have. The good feelings we generate will complete the circuit and voila! Manifestation!

Here's how that'll work:

## Attachment

If you want to change the way things are, the trick is to be unattached to the outcome. This is one big enigma, so let's take it apart.

What do we mean by "attachment"? Attachment is "I gotta have it and I suffer without it." "NEED" is the word I use for attachment, and one I prefer because it gets right to the heart of the matter. It's usually accompanied by some degree of fear, anger, anxiety, or frustration. Since we communicate with BOB through emotion, It gets the request, no matter what the emotion behind it.

When people are in NEED, they radiate "I don't have…" as that is the focus of their attention. They exude lack. Sometimes they're downright creepy. You can notice certain characteristics when somebody (maybe even you or me) is needy.

- They never get enough.
- They try to manipulate people and situations to get more.
- They're afraid they'll lose what they have.
- They envy those who have more than they do.
- They perceive other people only as threats to or suppliers of their need.

- When others get it more easily, it lowers their selfesteem.

In other words, they're putting out a lot of "I don't have" energy when they operate from NEED. Think how puny a positive affirmation is beside all that. NEED is another acronym. It stands for "Never Ending Expectations and Demands" and if it's there, it's active, often below the surface.

Just for fun, pretend you need money. If you're loaded, you probably know somebody else who really needs it. Go down the list above, and I'll bet you can remember times when they've done all that. What? You, too? Yeah, I know.

Now, suppose you're looking for a place to park your car at the mall.

All of a sudden, the list looks pretty silly, doesn't it? Who ever lost a single wink of sleep over not having a place to park? See? That's non-attachment. That's why one of the first things a student learns to create is a parking space. Just think a message to BOB of "I accept a place to park" and BOB makes sure somebody nearby is just about to leave.

Now try it with the rent, that perfect relationship, or something else you really must have. See? Now there's all that bulleted stuff above that comes into play, so it takes a little more work. Feeling "I need" is just another way to say, "I don't have," and BOB says "OK, you don't have."

On the other hand, "I accept." is just another way of saying, "I accept." If the NEED isn't there to interfere, the message from BOB is "OK, here it is" or "OK, it's on the way." If I say "I accept." when I'm really feeling "I need," it's back to square one. Remember, we're all part of BOB, so we might fool ourselves, but we can't fool BOB.

The list works for any emotional NEED. You went down the list thinking about you or someone you know who needs money. Try it now thinking of someone who is horny. See? It's still the same list, and it still actually repels what you need the most. The stronger the need, the more repulsive is the energy (and the needy one).

So where does BOB come in? Remember, It's just playing a game. We're all parts of BOB, so It gets to play the game from infinite perspectives. Heroes and horrors are all part of BOB's experience. The horrors are caught up to one degree or another in RACE Trap rules. They're either drowning in righteousness or floundering for approval.

The heroes, on the other hand, are those who work their way through the RACE Trap rules in varying degrees of realization and find the cardinal rule — the ONLY rule: Thoughts become things. I don't know about you, but I know for sure I'd rather be a hero than a horror so through me BOB can have the experience of winning the game in new and exciting ways.

## The Hero Mindset

Have you ever seen an unhappy winner? Of course not. It follows then, if you want to win at the game of life, be happy. Misery is for losers.

Yet there's the famous quotation by Henry Clay, "I would rather be right than President." Well, there are a lot of things I'd rather be than President … but that's beside the point. There's only one important thing to remember about that:

Henry Clay is dead.

Students of Logic 101 will denounce the above reasoning and they will be right. If you disapprove of my non sequiturs, I must confess:

I don't care.

I'll be happy anyhow.

So who's the winner?

Yes, it's nice to be right, but it's not a path to happiness. Once you've made it to happiness, being right doesn't matter. Love matters. It's the feeling we get when we give up the attachment to being right. The positive energy we radiate when we're happy is the energy of Love. We aren't worried about being right or getting anybody's approval.

Once filled with Love, we then create our lives in the best possible way. It's the deep-down sense of "I'm OK even if you disapprove of me," and "I'm OK even if my logic is absurd." "OK-ness" is the emotional foundation for creativity and happiness.

BOB doesn't care whether one part of It sees things differently than another, in fact It's fine with It if everybody has a different experience. Variety is the spice of BOB. We're just a bunch of little kids here to entertain BOB as we play in the sandbox of life.

Is BOB having fun? Of course It is. It now has millions... nay BILLIONS of units of Its own creation right here experiencing this game in millions... nay BILLIONS of different ways, from the horrors of the tortured to the ecstasies of the lovers; from the beauty of the symphony to the ugliness of the battlefield; from the naiveté of the followers to the mendacity of the leaders; from the generosity of the givers to the greed of the takers; from the sanctimony of the teacher to the gullibility of the student; from the piety of the priest to the guilt of the sinner; from love to hate and everything in between

Now, THAT'S entertainment!

We can choose how BOB entertains Itself

through us. Our life can be a horror story, adventure, drama, romance, or sitcom. The more love we enjoy, the more choices we have, and the closer we are to the essence of BOB.

So what's our part in all this? Simple. Our mission, our ONLY mission is to enjoy life as much as we can and use the creative power of BOB to make it more fun for everybody else, too. BOB will like that.

So will we.

Some may say my point of view is blasphemy, and they could be right.

I'll take the sitcom.

Speaking of sitcoms, it might be time to bring up the idea of worship. BOB, being unconditional Love, doesn't know ego, so how do you think all that hootin', hollerin', and hosanna affects It?

That's right. Not a bit, although there's no doubt It finds it entertaining.

How do you think It responds to words and thoughts like "I'm a miserable sinner." or, "I know my limitations." or "I'm unworthy?"

Probably in the only way It can respond: "YES, you're miserable." or "YES, you're limited." or "YES, you're unworthy." Remember, thought is creative and the word adds power to the thought. Add emotion, and voila! BOB always says, "YES."

On the other hand, "Halleluiah, I'm saved." or "BOB loves me." or "I'm going to Blissville." get the same responses: "YES, you're saved." or "YES, I love you." or "YES, you're going to Blissville." It all works. Think happy thoughts, and that's the experience you create.

See? BOB...Bliss... Unconditional Love... has no concept of "right" or "wrong." It's only what we create with our thoughts and it's all OK. It also has consequences and they all come together to entertain BOB.

Now, here's the kicker! No matter what we create, eventually we'll create something else. After all, we're eternal beings (like BOB) and eternity is a long, long time. It will come to pass for everybody that they'll realize the creative power of their thought and play a different game to entertain BOB in another way.

Let's take that one step further. There's no such thing as salvation. There's only thinking and doing something else. There's nothing to be saved from, other than what you think, and what you think will also save you. If you want to think you're saved, do so. You will be. If you want to think you're damned, do so. You will be.

Some day in the circumstances you create, you will have suffered enough and then what? You'll do something else... and we'll all eventually do something else and something else and something else. Eternity takes a while, y'know.

The heroes are those who discover and use the creative power of their thoughts — the ones who realize that thought powered by emotion is the creative force in the universe and who take charge of their thinking. They create happy lives for themselves and for the pleasure and entertainment of BOB. Eventually, we all are heroes. For some, it just takes a little longer.

What do you think?

## Onward

We've laid the theoretical groundwork and it was fun in the abstract. Now for the good news. It's a Power, It's real and you can use it. Like it or not, right now BOB is looking out through your eyes, feeling your feelings and thinking your thoughts.

What does It see? Does It look out on a beautiful world? Does it see a drama or conflict? Perhaps It sees real tragedy, or a comedy, or possibly just humdrum routine. That's OK, too. To BOB, it's just another view of Paradise.

What does It feel? Love? Joy? Fear? Anxiety? Worry? Guilt? Anger? Contentment? Boredom? Bliss? All that is OK, only some is more fun than others.

What does It think? Anticipation? Judging? Planning? Wishing? Thanking? Hoping? Judging? Condemning? Praising?... Ooops... I said "judging" twice. I wonder why.

BOB sees, feels, and thinks exactly what you see, feel, and think because it's all real! There is such an entity, It is infinite; It is powerful; It is intelligent and you (and I) are a part of It.

Do you realize what that means? It means our thought is creative, too. It means our dreams can translate into form if we just get rid of the RACE Trap stuff in the way. It means the happier we can live our lives, the greater the blessings of BOB are bestowed upon us... or more accurately, the greater the blessings of BOB we bestow upon ourselves.

The rest of this book is about how to clear away the debris and allow our thoughts to become things in the finest possible way.

# 4 WATCH YOUR MOUTH

*"Argue for your limitations and sure enough,
they're yours."*
*— Richard Bach*

The limitation you speak is the limitation you get. If we don't speak or think limitation our lives will truly be unlimited.

It isn't easy.

See? There goes another one. Why can't it be easy? Because I just said "It isn't easy." My little mind hears and sends the message to BOB which says, "Right, it isn't easy."

The spoken word is one of the most powerful tools we use to create our lives. It's most easily heard by our mind, which then sends the e-mail to BOB, which creates whatever life or limitations we request.

What comes out of the mouth also goes in the ears, and the ears have the mouth outnumbered. Just as we knocked out the walls of BOB's room, so must we knock out the walls of our limitations to enjoy the infinitude of goodies available to us.

Suppose, for example, I decide to put my hard-earned money into a risky business. It would be stress-ful, but I could become filthy rich.

Look how the modifiers limit my creation.

- I limit my avenues of abundance as I call my money "hard-earned."
- I limit my success as I call my business "risky."
- I limit my enjoyment as I call situations "stress-ful."
- I limit my income and self-respect as I call wealth "filthy."

Couldn't I put that money that comes to me so easily into an exciting business and breeze my way to vast wealth? Why not? BOB doesn't care. It just says, "Yes."

"Picky, picky" you may say, but so does BOB. It picks up every thought and word and delivers the goods — or the "not-so-goods" if that's what we say or think about.

### Righteousness and Approval Complicate Everything

Why, then, do we create all this limitation for ourselves? The answer boils down to one friendly old acronym, RACE; those RACE Trap rules we adopted when we thought we needed rules.

If we don't actually live the unlimited life at our command, there must be a reason. There is, but we'd rather mask it with excuses. Because of RACE Trap rules, we need to get those around us to agree and approve of our limited selves.

It's also likely that our friends face the same restrictions, and we may want to stick with them to "belong." Nothing bugs the limited mind as much as somebody who has made a change for the better.

We can usually find some degree of self-righteous justification or need for approval beneath the limitations we unconsciously accept. All the egos then get together to create the RACE Trap, that muck of limited thinking we have to wade through to be sure what we create is best for all.

Let's take another analogy. To make it easier to picture, we'll go back to the BOB room, filled wall to wall, floor to ceiling with BOB. Now picture in the room a little game of Whack-a-Mole — The game where air pressure makes moles pop out of holes and you try to hit them with a mallet before they disappear.

BOB plays Whack-a-Mole with us. Our thoughts are the moles, and BOB's mallet is YES! We pop up with a thought/request/statement and quick as a wink BOB hits it with the YES! "I'm prosperous." YES! "I can't afford it." YES! BOB's mallet never misses a mole. All moles are not created equal, and the equivalent of the air pressure that makes them pop up is the emotional charge behind the thought. For our purposes there are only two emotions: Love and fear. We do all we can to stimulate the positive feelings we call love.

BOB won't be fooled. You'll get a "YES" to what you REALLY believe. If a claim of "I am abundant" is negated by a fear of lack, what do you think will get the "YES"? If fear of being alone contradicts "I have a wonderful, beautiful, exciting, super duper, loving relationship", whom do you think you're kidding? Whack! Whack! YES! YES!

Naturally, when we go back and forth like that, there's a lot of starting and stopping. BOB doesn't care, It just whacks YES! It does get kinda hard on the mole after while, though.

Once again, let's remove the walls and expand BOB and the game board out to infinity. Now, there are an infinite number of moles and BOB has an infinite number of YES! mallets for infinite whacks.

Still, since all us moles are connected under the table, it's easy for BOB to move things around so we all get what we ask for, but it's helpful to give our requests as much emphasis as we can. Thus we speak our word. We hope BOB will hear us above the din as we make more din.

Actually, BOB gets the request when we think it, but speaking it aloud helps strengthen it in our minds, and since there's so much back-and-forth in our thinking, every little bit helps. The problem is sometimes the words we speak often work against us. Here are some of the ways we limit ourselves with our spoken (and sometimes sung) words.

Your life today is the result of your thinking of yesterday, thanks to BOB whacking you with YES! If you want it to be different tomorrow, you need to sow the seeds of thought today. The first step is to watch your language.

# 5 THE BIG THREE:
## Health, Money, Relationships

*Nothing plays a greater role in how we construct our fortunes and misfortunes than the thoughts we choose to think.*
*— Mike Dooley*

## How to Avoid Good Health

When confronted with symptoms or illness, most of us find it hard to declare perfection in the midst of apparent imperfection. Pretty soon, some are convinced this stuff doesn't work and they're sick of trying.

Notice anything?

One of the most common declarations of limitation is in our unconscious use of common phrases. How many times a day do we say we're sick of this or tired of that, or just plain sick and tired? Do you think repeating it over and over will make you healthy and energetic?

The trick in physical healing is to MAINTAIN your picture of perfect health, regardless of what's right before your eyes. That way, the only thing BOB can whack YES! to is that picture of wholeness. It requires constant denial of limited thinking especially if you have doctors who think they're BOB.

How's your lumbago today? Are your allergies acting up? Are you handling your drinking problem? What about your high cholesterol?

Do all these things REALLY belong to you?

Be careful about taking possession of something you don't want. When you speak of your disease, here comes BOB with the YES! That's right, it's yours. As long as you own it, you can't get rid of it.

We buy into a lot of limiting beliefs when we think about food. There is nothing you can eat that somebody wouldn't tell you is not healthy. There's plenty of agreement to the proposition "if it tastes good, it must be bad for you." Limiting beliefs about health are just that—limiting beliefs, which can be overcome. Why should limiting beliefs about food be any different?

If people believe their food choices are healthy, so it will be for them. If they believe my food choices are not healthy, they've overstepped their bounds. My own belief system extols the gastronomical benefits of a good filet mignon. My taste buds stand up and applaud the savory blend of onions, grease, and "whatever" found only within the buns of White Castle burgers.

Visualizing health and energy is helpful. So is affirmation. I could go on in great detail about the benefits of all this, but I'm tired of preaching to you.

Oooops!

## How to Stay Poor

Money is another area where we get a lot of whacks from BOB, and it's well deserved. After a session of affirmations and visualizations of a lifestyle of unlimited abundance, it's off to the grocery where we buy what's on sale and complain about the price of gas.

Of course, there's nothing wrong with buying on

sale, but your test of consciousness is whether or not you'd buy it if it were full price. If you're shopping for something and find it on sale, it's a nice surprise. If you see a reduced price and buy the item because it's on sale, your prosperity thinking might need work.

Don't you just love yard sales? Everything's on sale. How do you approach them? Do you go with the idea of getting what you want as cheaply as you can and haggle for the last penny? Or do you anticipate a nice surprise to find something you never knew you wanted? When you focus on the prize instead of the price, you're thinking is prosperous and you gain new levels of pleasure from the adventure. You can still haggle if you want, but for the fun of the game, not out of lack.

We have a society that promotes poverty as a virtue. Robin Hood is a hero because he stole from the rich and gave to the poor. Churches idolize poverty as they collect for their treasure troves. We call the wealthy "lucky" and those with less "unfortunate" as if their own effort or consciousness has nothing to do with their state.

Movies portray anybody of great wealth as the bad guy and the poor kid from the other side of the tracks always gets the girl. The poor person is always "hard-working." The wealthy get "unearned income" and nobody ever wanted to tax the poor.

As the saying goes, "It's no shame to be poor, but it's no great honor either."

What can you do to counter the daily tsunami of poverty adulation? The first step is to purge your mind of any idea that there's something wrong or immoral about being rich. Think of the wealthy as inspiring rather than conniving. Oh sure, there are rich scoundrels just as there are poor ones, but because one crook is rich it doesn't follow that all rich people are crooks.

The next point is to remember we're all made out of the stuff of BOB, and none of us are more or less worthy than anybody else. Your thought creates your world, no matter what you think. The same goes for everybody else.

We live in an infinitely abundant universe and you're entitled to as much as you can accept. The river doesn't care if you come for water with a thimble, a bucket, or a tank truck. If you really believe you're poor, your thoughts are your thimble. If, without unconscious doubts, you know you rate vast wealth, your mind is your tank truck. Most of us are in the bucket class.

It's up to you to police your mind and rid it of thoughts of poverty and lack. Here are some of the common expressions we use that can get in the way of our prosperity consciousness: Of course "I can't afford it" is popular, especially when you really mean "I have higher priorities for my money."

Do you see wealthy people as "filthy rich?" Unless you're into filth, you might want to start viewing them as "wonderfully abundant." What about them paying their "fair share"? What's "fair?" The answer is usually "More for me." Notice that people who want others to pay a "fair share" generally want to be on the receiving end.

And what about that awful phrase "hard-earned money." Remember, BOB is right there with the "YES" for when you think or say "hard earned." Why can't "easy money" be just as virtuous?

Look. BOB doesn't care if you're rich or poor. It gets Its entertainment expressing through you no matter what drama you create for yourself. BOB just says "Yes" to whatever you think or say. Your life right now is the culmination of your past thinking. Keep thinking the same way and you'll keep getting the same thing.

Some people say this is unrealistic. On the contrary, it's completely realistic in the Mind of BOB. The problem is our belief that "reality" is limited to the physical. Did you ever notice when people say, "Be realistic," they're usually saying, "Be negative"?

When thoughts or words of limitation come to the fore, be positive:

Just say, "No."

## How to Avoid Happy Relationships

How do we limit ourselves by what we say about relationships?

We all are taught we need to find Mr. or Ms. "Right." Somewhere "out there" is your Soul Mate, the only one for you — your Prince (or Princess) Charming. If the planets are properly aligned, and you hit the right bars, and you do everything right, there's a slim chance that maybe, perhaps, possibly, someday you might find each other and the sparks will fly. Meanwhile, keep on hoping and kissing frogs.

How's that working for you?

Think for a moment of all the potential partners you meet or have met during your "available" years. Perhaps a hundred? Maybe even a couple of hundred?

Considering all the people there are in your city, or in the whole country, the odds against finding "the one" are pretty foreboding. Could it be that the idea that there's only one person in the world for you might be a limiting belief? There sure are a lot of people paired off that tells me the odds are much better than that.

What if you were to approach money with the same attitudes we learn about relationships? There'll be only one dollar in the world for you and if you're lucky enough to find "Dollar Charming" you'd better hold onto it because you'll probably never find another one. Maybe you can get it to commit to staying in your wallet forever. How silly.

How did we ever get the idea that love was so scarce when it's the very stuff we're made of?

Do you think Mr. Right has something to do with "Right"? After all, nobody is looking for Mr. Wrong. Mr. Right has to look right, think right, do right, dress right and smell right. He must have the right job and bank account to match, and come from the right side of the tracks. He must also gain the approval of friends before achieving full status. Once again the RACE Trap enters the picture. **R**ighteousness and **A**pproval **C**omplicate **E**verything.

The same holds true for seekers of "Ms. Right" of course, but because of their BOB-given libidos, men don't seem to be as choosy.

How did we get that way? Can you say, "Cinderella?" Talk about reaching out for limitation! Scrub enough floors and you too may find a fairy BOBmother to send you to the ball where you'll meet the prince. The story ends before you find out who cleans up after his horse.

Do you see now why we say, "All the good ones are taken?" It's just one more argument for limitation.

How do you think relationships will be different if we come from an abundant point of view?

Perhaps the first welcome casualty of an abundance consciousness would be the dreaded "c" word. If you believe in abundance of love, every "Mr. Right" is "Mr. Right Now," even if it's the same person for the rest of your life.

So many seek commitment out of fear of being alone in the future that they mess up their "now" and wind up in the very state they fear. On the other hand, if you can make your present moment happy, you won't need a guarantee for the future.

Coming from abundance is one way to do it. If you approach relationships with a sense of plenty, you won't be driven by a fear of loss, and you'll be more fun to be around. Thus all your relationships will be better without hardly trying.

How often have you said (or heard), "This isn't going anywhere." Relationships don't have wheels. When you live in abundance, it's already "there," so you might as well relax and enjoy it.

Which brings us to the oft' desired "c" word — Communication. If we had an abundant view of relationships, communication wouldn't be the big deal we make it into because most of the time we don't share because of fear. I'm afraid we'll start a fight, or I'm afraid I'll hurt your feelings, or I'm afraid you'll leave... All based on righteousness, approval, and scarcity in that order.

When you overcome the need to be right, there's nothing to fight over. When you overcome the need for approval, you can communicate more directly, and when you overcome feelings of scarcity you don't have to worry about being alone. Everything works better.

# 6 DOWN WITH NEGATIVITY

*"Accentuate the positive; eliminate the negative"*
*— Johnny Mercer*

Remember, the Being of Bliss (BOB) is not a person. It's an Essence. It's Life, It's Intelligence, and It's Love. With our limited vision, it's easy to give It a human face and ascribe human characteristics to It.

For instance, you may say, "It's BOB's will" when something happens, as if this Infinite Power cares about your every move. To say something like "BOB wants me to be an accountant" is like saying "Electricity wants me to have a blender."

BOB is a power, not a person and doesn't care if you're a lawyer or a garbage collector (although one may appear more dignified than the other). To BOB there's no difference, because It experiences life through both.

We each create our life with our thoughts as we consciously or unconsciously plug into that power. Within the space of BOB's creativity, as we trek our way through this life, BOB responds to our creative thoughts in the direction of maximum enjoyment all around.

So why isn't it always fun? The answer is the RACE Trap (**R**ighteousness and **A**pproval **C**omplicate

Everything). When our thinking is colored by a need to be right or need for approval, BOB gets Its entertainment by living our drama. Although It may prefer enjoyment, the basic rule "Thoughts become things" takes precedence and BOB always gets entertainment.

There is a difference between entertainment and enjoyment. Although a horror movie might be entertaining, we might not enjoy it. War, famine, and pestilence can be a form of entertainment. Enjoyable? Unlikely. Entertaining? Always.

For example, suppose I'm working on my prosperity as many of us are. When I focus on my abundant life, opportunities arise for me to provide something of value that will not only increase my prosperity, but make a positive contribution to the experience of other expressions of BOB.

If, on the other hand, I focus on my lack, I may get desperate and rob the corner bank to alleviate it. There will be consequences. Perhaps I'll learn from it and seek my wealth in a way that works better once I get out on parole.

Or I may not. BOB doesn't care, and I'll get to do it over (and take the consequences) until I get it right. Multiply me by billions, and we have the current world situation. All of us are trying to get back to Love in our own way and trapping ourselves in multiple degrees of the RACE Trap. What's a feller to do?

## Positive Thinking

It seems to me if we purge the negative (RACE) thoughts and surge the positive ones, the outcome will always be better. The next line of the song quoted at the beginning of this chapter is, "Don't mess with Mr. In-Between." What's in-between creative thoughts and positive outcome? What else but the RACE Trap?

What we need to do is to recognize and deny those sneaky thoughts that limit us, and replace them with others that lead more toward the life we want.

In *The One Minute Manager*, Kenneth Blanchard advises us to catch people doing something right and praise them for it to reinforce the desired behavior. This is also an effective method with children, or even spouses. However, if we do the same with BOB, we will reinforce our own positive attitude, which will let us create our lives better, and easier. It's called "the attitude of gratitude."

It's easy to catch BOB doing something right because It really can't do anything wrong. That's why BOB's BOB.

BOB is an impersonal abstract force and it seems a little silly to say, "Thanks, BOB." Yet we don't do it for BOB, we do it for ourselves. It creates the emotional voltage to help our thoughts build our world in the best possible way. You can't feel bad and grateful at the same time.

## Gratitude

Early in the morning, I'd plan my "things to do" for the day. One day I realized I wasn't planning things to do, I was planning things to fix. I'd look around my world, see what was wrong or needed fixing and before I knew it I was buried in my own complaints.

It made a difference when I created "Gratitude Time." Now early in the morning, I spend time with "Thanks, BOB." Then I see how long I can go before I find something to complain about. My goal is to make it to 10:00 a.m. It really works well, especially when I sleep late.

So when you come across something you like, and especially if it's something you consciously created before, don't forget to say, "Thanks, BOB." BOB doesn't care about your manners, but the emotional force of your gratitude adds energy to your declaration and just helps everything get better and better.

Let's go back to our prosperity example to see how it works. Suppose my four-figure bank account has two of the figures on the wrong side of the decimal point. This reality is the result of my thinking, conscious or unconscious, in the past.

If, upon seeing this, my first thought is "I'm broke," then I create more of the same. Good ole BOB with Its Whack-a-Mole "Yes." Not only is my "brokeness" put forth with my thoughts, but also with the power behind it of whatever I might be feeling ... perhaps something like despair, frustration, fear, panic.... You remember those.

On the other hand, if my immediate reaction denies the appearance, or rather the reality I created in the past, then the creative force I put forward is "I'm prosperous." It's a bit of a trick to look at the little bank account and declare prosperity, but that's why it's called denial. This is where gratitude comes in. It's the motive force behind our declaration so BOB can whack a big "Yes."

Then when things start to get a little better, more gratitude pushes the process along and strengthens all our declarations. Of course we have to keep it up, since BOB whacks "Yes" to every thought, but the gratitude keeps it coming in the best possible way, so I won't have to rob that bank after all.

## Affirmation

If we hold that thought constantly and deeply enough it works its way into our Belief System so it creates the way we want it, even when we aren't looking. That's the power of affirmations.

The one thing to remember about affirmations, which are simply positive statements repeated regularly, is to think and affirm in the present tense. If you think, "Money is coming to me," by the time the future gets here, money will be coming to you, just as you thought. On the other hand, should you declare, "I have plenty of money," how different could be your situation upon arrival of the future?

Think positive, because negative thinking works.

# 7 THE SMALL STUFF

*"We are what we repeatedly do."*
*— Aristotle*

BOB has a problem.

Its nature is creative, Its power is creative, and yet many folks try to create more than they can accept, so they think BOB deserted them. That's not the case. BOB responds to what they *really* think.

## Think Small!

One of the first things we learn as we study mental cause is "Think big." However, if we affirm millions and have a "next month's rent" consciousness, we get the rent. We may speak the words for millions, but we don't really believe it (yet). You can't fool BOB.

How then can we stretch our consciousness? Think small. Little things are easier to accept and easier to bring about. That's why we get parking spaces more easily than that great relationship.

One thing that gets in the way of thinking small is we don't want to "bother" BOB with our puny requests. This is because we originally conceived of BOB in our image. That's mental residue that still thinks BOB is a guy (or gal) somewhere doling out favors. Tain't so. BOB's thing is to make stuff, It doesn't care what.

It's like saying "I won't turn on the lamp because I don't want to bother electricity." How silly.

In the universe of infinity, there is no "big" or "small". To BOB, it's as easy to send Prince Charming as it is to create a parking space. Both provide enjoyment for BOB through each of us, and it's only a matter of our individual ability to accept that makes the difference.

Every little thing we create with thought gives us another chance to say, "This stuff really works." What do you think BOB says then?

Exactly.

So whenever you drive somewhere, anticipate a safe, smooth drive (and a parking space). When you go to a restaurant, consciously accept good food and service. At a party, picture happy times and good friends.

Visualize cordiality and harmony at a business meeting. If you want to break into traffic, accept a safe opportunity. If you fly, accept on-time flights and thin, congenial seatmates.

With any of the little things, we instinctively know the world won't end if we don't get it. If we aren't hooked on it, we don't radiate lack, and there's no emotional conflict in our thinking. BOB gets a clear message, so It just says "Yes" as usual.

Get the idea? The little things strengthen our faith for the larger ones, and BOB is happy to oblige.

## Procrastinate Tomorrow

BOB created space and time to give us some interesting side effects — We call them "Yesterday" and "Tomorrow." Mix 'em in with the righteousness and approval of the RACE Trap, and we have new dimensions of experience for BOB.

Add yesterday and we have pride, nostalgia, guilt, and remorse. Add a bit of tomorrow and BOB gets to know hope, anticipation, worry, and dread. Then we get to live out our dramas however we want with justassoonases. Here are a few of them:

I'll be happy justassoonas —
…I graduate
…I get a car
…I move out
…I have a girlfriend (boyfriend)
…I get my degree
…I get a good job
…I get a promotion
…I get married
…I have kids
…I make more money
…the kids are grown
…I can dump this loser
…I get married again
…I retire
…I get to Heaven
…I reincarnate into a better life.

The big problem with the justassoonases is they're always changing, so what happens? You graduate and still aren't happy, so you get a car and you still aren't happy, so you move out and still aren't happy… and on and on.

Happiness is NOW…. In fact, EVERYTHING is NOW, and when a justassoonas becomes a NOW you discover you're still a mess. Of course, BOB just smacks you with another YES! and it's onward to the next justassoonas.

How many justassoonases will it take to be happy? Let BOB count the ways. Of course, the answer is "none."

Happiness is in the place between yesterday and tomorrow called NOW. A wise man (Ken Keyes) once said, "If you can't be happy here and now, what makes you think you'll be happy ten minutes from now — or ten years from now?"

That sounds nice, but how do we go about it? Remember the real rule of the game: Thoughts become things. If your mind dwells in the past, you re-create your past. If your mind dwells in the future, you put out the energy for a justassoonas.

Pop quiz: Where do you focus your mind if you want to create happiness NOW?

Right!

## SHAZAM! This Moment

Look around you right now. Quick! Find something to appreciate. SHAZAM! You're in the moment.

Think of something in the future you're worried about.

Look around you right now. Quick! Find something to appreciate. SHAZAM! You're in the moment.

Think of something from the past you feel guilty over.

Look around you right now. Quick! Find something to

appreciate. SHAZAM! You're in the moment.

The word SHAZAM!, incidentally, is the magic word that transforms an ordinary person into a superhero. When little Billy Batson spoke it in the comic book, a bolt of lightning transformed him into the mighty Captain Marvel. I find it a convenient metaphor.

Whenever I'm faced with a problem or obstacle, I can say SHAZAM! Quick as lightning I focus my attention back in my now, feel appreciation, connect with BOB, and become the superhero that can solve any problem and conquer any limitation. I may not fly off and fight bad guys, but I can surely get the instant inspiration I need or help from BOB to move along. Remember, thoughts become things.

You don't believe SHAZAM!? OK, then it won't work for you. What do you think will?

# 8 DON'T WORRY – BE HAPPY

*Worry never robs tomorrow of its sorrow,*
*it only saps today of its joy.*
*— Leo Buscaglia*

## Don't Worry About Worrying

Worry is the direct opposite of justassoonas, only we anticipate disaster instead of delight. The difference is that fear is usually stronger than hope and BOB is standing by waiting to bop us with a YES! Remember Job: "That which I have feared the most has come upon me."

Some may say, "Of course worrying works. Whatever I worry about doesn't happen." To which I reply, "Are you sure?" Some people I know are "professional worriers." They constantly worry about some awful thing about to happen to them, and it often does. Even if that specific worried thing doesn't happen, it tells BOB that they are worried, and of course, BOB whacks YES and they have more to be worried about.

I worked in an office once with one such person. Her life was a move from one disaster to another. Her car got broken into, as did her house at a different time.

When she tried to do anything at all, she was so worried about making a mistake that it took her twice as long and still the results were amazingly inept. One time when most of the people were in a company meeting, she came into my office upset that nobody was there. She thought it was a bomb scare.

The poor thing didn't work there very long, but we often remarked about what a sad example she was of the truth of the statement, "Thoughts become things." It's as if she came with her own private rain cloud.

Another individual I knew often worried so much about his plans working out perfectly, that he'd covered all the bases in triplicate ... and still ran into extraordinary difficulty as he moved through his drama.

The key is to trust. BOB doesn't want to create disaster for anyone. People do that well enough on their own. On the contrary BOB wants to have fun through us, and It always sets us up to win.

Remember, BOB's only emotion is Love, and part of the game is to express the Love of BOB. Naturally, BOB will always arrange things to honor our requests in the best possible way.

The problem is people don't know this, so they regularly choose to lose as they try to arrange things without trusting BOB.

BOB has motive, means, and opportunity. It has the motive to experience fun and winning. Since everything is made out of BOB and It has the power to manipulate everything, It naturally has the means, and since it's always now, It always has the opportunity. So what's not to trust?

SHAZAM!

Let go and let BOB.

## Not Guilty

If there's anything more useless than worrying about something that might happen, it's worrying about something that has already happened. There's a name for that, too. It's called "guilt."

Guilt is a marvelous hook for manipulation and control, because there's no way anybody can go back and redo whatever it is they feel guilty about. Mothers, churches, and politicians are masters of the "art." They might say, "Be a good boy (girl), put a nickel on the plate, or vote for me and I'll assuage your guilt for a little while."

Note that they only offer to ease your guilt for a little while, not rid you of it completely, because then they wouldn't be able to control you any more. The only way out is to forgive yourself for whatever it is you feel guilty about. Remember BOB – Unconditional Love.

SHAZAM!

The verdict is in. NOT GUILTY!

## Delightful Surprises

It's another beautiful day in paradise!

This is one of my favorite expressions, and a useful observation for Monday morning, sudden showers, and flat tires. It's a way to handle life's little disasters that aren't really disasters.

You might not immediately use paradise to describe your situation. But when you make the statement, BOB whacks it and it's one more particle in favor of Paradise over Purgatory. Chances are it'll be more fun than "Welcome to Hell."

Like SHAZAM!, it also can bring us into the moment and before we know it, we can appreciate the world around us just as it is, and it's a prelude to Delightful Surprises, those little serendipities that happen all the time but often sneak by without proper recognition.

A word or two about Delightful Surprises. I live among them as much as I can, as BOB knows better than I what will delight me and what will surprise me. Surprises can only happen here and now, so I try to acknowledge and appreciate them on the spot. Not only does it keep me conscious of my own position as a part of BOB, but also it keeps me open to receive more. SHAZAM! Another delightful surprise!

Have you ever gone outdoors on a partly cloudy day and wished the sun would come out, only to have the clouds part at just the right moment? What a delightful surprise!

Have you ever driven down the street and caught every light green? There's another delightful surprise. Have you ever driven down a two-lane road behind a large truck? Isn't it a delightful surprise to have it there to run interference? Delightful surprises are often a matter of how we choose to view them.

Have you ever had a question in your mind and randomly opened a book to the answer? Are you delighted and surprised? Yep, another one.

Don't you love it when you're out and about and run into a friend you hadn't expected to be there? Sure enough, delightful surprises are everywhere.

How about a surprise piece of music that brings pleasant memories into the here and how? Delightful, isn't it!

I could go on and on about this, but I won't.

Isn't that a delightful surprise?!

# 9 TIME FOR FUN

*"The purpose of morality is to teach you, not to suffer and die, but to enjoy yourself and live."*
*— Ayn Rand*

## Be Unique, Like Everybody Else

Isn't it interesting that this Spiritual insight should be so well presented by a renowned Atheist? I believe it just underscores the essence of our individuality. Since our purpose is to provide BOB with entertainment through each of us, our road to happiness is to celebrate our uniqueness in every way we can.

People are always saying things like "Be yourself," and I've always wondered, "What the hell does that mean?" Since I am one of the avenues through which BOB expresses and we're all here for Its entertainment I certainly want to be as much of myself as possible ... whatever that is.

*"Why didn't they repeal inhibition while they were at it?"* said the wonderful James Thurber. You can't "be yourself" if you're inhibited by either righteousness or need for approval. Remember, BOB is only Love, and RACE Trap rules exist only to make the game interest-

ing for It.

It follows then, that if you suppress whatever you want to do out of fear of doing it wrong then you won't enjoy yourself and you will deprive BOB of Its pleasure as well. The same holds true with inhibitions based upon "What will people think?"

That translates into the idea that if you hold back and "behave," not only do you miss out on the pleasure, but you cheat BOB as well. So, next time you have an impulse to do something unexpected or un-characteristic, give it a try. It can't hurt.

Of course, you also want to make sure it can't hurt anybody else as well. It's all BOB, you know.

Another way you might keep from "being your-self" is to identify with your stuff. It's amazing how often I'm parked near the entrance to wherever I'm going.

Even more amazing is the fact that it's really my car parked there. I'm someplace else.

Gotcha!

An interesting exercise is to write down several different answers to the question "Who am I?"

When you get to "A unique expression of BOB" you win the prize.

In fact, you ARE the prize, so flaunt your hid-den talents.

## Plan Something Spontaneous

I like reruns. They don't take any energy or thought. I know what's coming and how they're going to end. They're great after a day's work where I can fall asleep, go unconscious, or totally ignore them secure in the knowledge I'm not missing anything.

BOB, on the other hand, has seen enough reruns, and because I am an outlet for Its expression, if I replay any situations from the past, somehow I feel as if I'm letting BOB down since It's getting entertainment through me. Disappointment is impossible, of course, since BOB doesn't care. It just wants to be entertained.

It follows, then, to be true stewards of this life; it falls upon us to make it interesting. If you'll pardon a reference to musical theatre, we can "Open a new window every day."

Many people make their relationships into re-runs where the next relationship looks and sounds like the one before. The name and face may be different, but the drama is the same. How can you expect to have a different partner when you still have the same head?

It's similar with parents and children, just different dramas. But as long as we think the same way, we get the same thing and fall into the world of justassoonas.

How about that job? Is every workplace occupied by the same annoying incompetents? What about your life? Is it always the same old routine? Are you bored? Are you in a rut? Remember, a rut is just a grave without the ends.

## Goof Off Day

Every now and then, I take a spontaneous day just to goof off.

My only rules are that I can't do anything related to my regular routine, and can only do things I enjoy.

I'd go to the zoo, take a drive in the country, play Frisbee in the park, or even un-clutter a shelf or two or maybe sweep out the garage. Can you imagine a whole day away from e-mail? Talk about living in the moment!

You might find other pastimes more suitable for

you. BOB just wants you to enjoy it so It can enjoy your special life through you.

I've always thought it was sad that people have to lie and call in "sick," just to take an extra day off. Wouldn't it be nice to call in "healthy" and take the day off?

Who knows? It might even be a springboard to a better job.

Just don't say I sent you.

## Intuition

Did you ever say anything like:

"I don't know why. It just 'feels' right."

"I knew I should have taken that road."

"I had a feeling it was something important."

"I knew I shouldn't have thrown that out."

Or anything similar? That's what we call "intuition." A cruder description might be "gut feeling." Others might call it a "hunch," and holy holies could call it "Divine Guidance." I call it BOB's signpost.

Every thought we have every moment goes into BOB's creation pool to mingle with the thoughts of everybody else, and the creative energy goes forth to materialize the consensus of the moment. We could get a clearer idea if we were consistent, but we aren't, so there's a lot of static.

Every now and then, we get a glimpse of our direction, but usually there's so much chatter in our minds it quickly gets obscured. There are ways however, depending upon your belief system (B.S.) to "read" the signpost. One popular way is to visit a psychic.

A psychic will attune to the force you put out and attempt to offer predictions and guidance for your life. This is perfectly reasonable since we're all BOB anyhow, but when the psychic tunes in to your signpost, it's read through his/her own belief system and emphasis. This often renders the advice of limited value or completely useless.

The opposite can also be an influence. I once had a psychic acquaintance whom I knew was prone to predict disasters, and he warned me about a car breakdown about to happen. Because I knew of his particular orientation, I casually ignored his warning.

The car broke down of course, but it was merely one step on the way to getting a vehicle strong enough to take me across the country.

It was not a disaster at all, but had I fully bought into his prediction and the tone of it, it would have been much more troubling than it was. I didn't even know I needed a stronger vehicle until I was halfway home.

You're always better off if you can read your own signpost, unfettered by the beliefs and prejudices of somebody else. Of course, this takes a little more discipline than merely stopping by the sign of the upraised palm, but that way you just have your own B.S. to put aside.

The best way I've found to do this is through meditation. Meditation is more than just sitting quietly, sifting through your troubles, or contemplating your day's activities. It's about actively being passive. It's about getting through the noise of righteousness and approval, then quieting the ancillary chatter in order to perceive the "still small voice" of BOB's direction.

The first meditation I ever learned was *Transcendental Meditation*, and it has served me well. It involves mentally repeating a single word that takes your attention off the intruding thoughts to leave room for intuition to come forth. It also has a positive physical effect, but that's just a bonus.

The "mantra" in TM is a Sanskrit word, but since

I don't speak Sanskrit, it just sounds like a nonsense word to me. That's all OK... it does the job. Some focus on a word like "love" or "forgiveness" or some other subject. That also works as will just about anything that allows you to become a spectator to your thoughts and bring forth your intuitive guidance. Other systems of meditation may be different on the surface, but all have similar goals.

Intuition isn't limited to times of meditation. I often have hunches and have learned to follow them. That includes immediately leaving a function after driving across town to get there. It includes taking a course of action that, on the surface, appeared inadvisable. It includes changing plans at the last minute just because it "felt" good to do it.

Remember, BOB experiences life through each of us, and BOB likes happy endings, so you can be sure your intuition will always lead in the direction of happiness and expansion.

# 10 YOUR CREATIVE MAP

*"Curtain up. Light the lights. You've got nothing to hit*
*but the heights!"*
*— Stephen Sondheim - Gypsy*

Now that you're developing all those good thought habits to help you avoid the RACE Trap, (Curtain up) it's time to use the power of BOB (Light the Lights) to bring what you want into your experience (the Heights). You'll do that with the Creative MAP.

Oh Nooooo! Not another acronym! Yep, but you'll love it because it tells exactly how to produce anything you want in life.

Think about it. Can you really believe it's simple to change your life with a three-letter acronym? Well, you'd better believe it, because that's the first step… and the last, come to think of it, because your B.S. (Belief System) controls everything. If you've come this far, we can assume you're ready.

By "ready" I don't mean you've achieved any degree of holiness, any more than I have. I simply mean you know the way it is with BOB and are on your way doing what you can with what you've got. It's all a journey and we're somewhere along the road. … But it's easier with a MAP.

You always put out creative energy that shapes your individual world, and a lot of the shape depends upon the emotion behind it. You want to manage your creativity so you like the result. The "normal" folk have different names for it—prayer, affirmation, treatment. All those words are fine and all work. They pray to get an answer, affirm to get a result, and treat for a demonstration. We MAP to get to a Destination.

Remember, it's all B.S. and really just different words to describe the same activity... consciously turning thoughts into things. MAP is simple and it helps remember. It also fits well with BOB. Here it is:

**Merge** (with BOB), **Appreciate** (SHAZAM!), **Picture** (the destination).

It's that simple.

## Merge

As we now know, BOB is everywhere and everything... including you and me. Yet we have so much chatter going on in our heads, that we often forget. Now as you develop your new habits it gets easier, but the mind is still busy as it creates every single minute of your life, whether you are conscious or unconscious.

You're already a part of BOB, so you may wonder how you can "merge," and with what? When you merge, you acknowledge your oneness and bring it to the forefront of your mind. You declare those attributes of BOB you want to be prominent at your destination and acknowledge that essence within you.

As an actor, when I'm about to go on stage, I prepare. I think about my character and "call forth" the traits I want to project in the scene. I could be the kindly old grandfather, self-centered antagonist, or village idiot. All those traits are within me. I just focus on the ones I want to use (some are easier than others).

It's the same way when we merge with BOB. We bring into consciousness those aspects we want to apply to our particular situation. In a sense, we "plug in" to the power.

There's no complete "list" of attributes of BOB where you can pick one from Column "A" and one from Column "B". We know BOB's basic nature is Love and Bliss and Its goal is maximum enjoyment expressing as each of us, so we just figure what would bring that into our situation and acknowledge our unity with it. Since BOB is everything anyhow, you can't make a wrong choice.

If, for example, you MAP for physical healing, you may focus on Life, Perfection, Circulation, Energy — whatever you want to manifest. If you MAP for personal relationships, you could focus on Harmony, Love, or Peace. Prosperity would have you merging with abundance and infinite supply.

Get the idea? Call forth whatever attributes you want, and let them fill your being. Take whatever time you need to actually get the feeling of it. Then you're ready for the next step.

## Appreciate

Appreciation is big power behind your communication with the Infinite Intelligence of BOB. It's often overlooked, or added by rote as an afterthought. Emotion is the force, and gratitude is a very special form of love. Gratitude and fear don't co-exist, and it's often fear that drives you to MAP in the first place. Your objective in the Appreciation phase is to wash away the fear.

Gratitude is a powerful emotion, and it doesn't matter what you're grateful for. BOB isn't your grandma waiting for a thank-you note. It couldn't care less, but it's YOUR feelings of gratitude that set the tone of your request.

Remember SHAZAM!. Find something to appreciate. You can be grateful for a beautiful sunny day as you MAP for a new job. You don't have to be thankful for the job that hasn't yet materialized. That's a little tricky, and it's a point of departure from conventional metaphysics, but it's the feeling that comes from gratitude and appreciation that counts.

I once had a copy of Rembrandt's Aristotle Contemplating the Bust of Homer prominently displayed in my living room. I honored that every time I walked by, as I appreciated all three of those guys.

Now I have pictures of my family, a piece of fine music, even a yummy candy bar, or my computer — that electronic cornucopia of multiple blessings. I can be grateful for it all, without even leaving my chair — my very comfortable chair. Ah, something else to appreciate. It's EVERYWHERE!

Get the idea? Anything you can do to whip up "that loving feeling" will send your creative thoughts to the Mind of BOB for the best possible destination. When gratitude overpowers fear, you're ready for the last step in the process.

## Picture

Here you are, merged with the BOB qualities and awash with gratitude. Now visualize yourself at the destination as vividly as you can—the destination, not the trip.

If wealth is your destination, picture yourself living that lifestyle. Don't just "wish" it... A wish is just another way of describing what you don't have. Visualize yourself in the situation where the wish has come true. Close your eyes and look around. Feel the feelings. Read that bank statement. Buy that plane ticket. Throw that party. Celebrate your wealth! Ain't it grand!

Keep the feeling going… Remember, emotion is the fuel that gets you to the destination.

If you're mapping to health, you may picture yourself dancing for joy with plenty of energy and stamina, or delighting over the way whatever wasn't working when you started now works. Visualize your immune system devouring little infections. Bones solid, organs functioning efficiently and yourself thrilled with the whole process.

Perhaps your MAP leads to happy relationships. For love relationships, clichés are always fun to picture. Running together through fields of clover, walking in the rain on the beach. Drinking Champagne from a slipper. Family relationships might have you mentally acting out "Leave It To Beaver" or "The Waltons." Picture business and social relationships in the best possible way.

WARNING! Don't try to figure out how to get there. BOB knows the roads better than you, and you certainly don't want to limit It. Remember our analogy of BOB with the satellite view.

Don't get too specific. Remember BOB knows the best thing and has the power to bring it to you. If that relationship MUST be Geraldine next door, she might have other plans. But BOB knows a better match, so be sufficiently open in your picturing to let the better one in. Otherwise, Geraldine's plans might neutralize yours. Her thoughts are creative too, y'know.

Or maybe Geraldine's plans mesh with yours; only your MAP doesn't consider her drinking problem. BOB knows of course, but since Geraldine is what you ask for, Geraldine is what you get, warts and all.

It's just like parking spaces. Any space that fits your desires would be fine. The occupant of that particular space in front of the door might not be ready to leave yet, but there's one nearby with time on the meter. BOB is full of delightful surprises. Be sure to leave room for them.

Go for the feeling. Do everything you can to generate the good feelings of arrival. If your destination is a new job, picture yourself satisfied, productive and prosperous, looking forward to a bright future. Imagine a comfortable place to work, surrounded by congenial and supportive colleagues.

Don't picture a specific job with a specific company. That's Geraldine with her warts. Picture the best possible outcome for you and rejoice in it. Remember, it's BOB's game, and BOB just wants to have fun as It expresses through you as you. Steer clear of the RACE Trap and arrival is assured.

Remember, don't be hooked on the outcome. Review Chapter III about attachment.

Woo Hoo!

You've merged with the Force of BOB and called for the attributes you want to emphasize.

You've nourished your sense of appreciation and filled your heart with gratitude.

You've pictured yourself at the destination and feel the good feelings of arrival.

Now what?

Nothing. You're finished. Let it go. Release it. Say "Amen" or "And so it is" or "Woo Hoo" to send it on its way for BOB to prepare the path.

Then, when the opportunity presents itself, or the "coincidence" happens, or you get that irresistible urge to do something, DO IT! Take action toward your destination, even if you don't know where that particular act will lead.

Your life will only get better, and BOB will be well entertained.

It loves happy endings.

Here's one of them now.

# ABOUT THE AUTHOR

Gregg Sanderson  has a rare view of the meta-physical universe. He traveled the road from Christian Science through Judaism, Agnosticism, Atheism, Living Love, Psychic Development, Spiritualism, Teaching of the Inner Christ, all the way to Science of Mind where he is a licensed practitioner. He is the author of *What Ever Happened To Happily Ever After?* and *Split Happens - Easing the Pain of Divorce.*

www.ingramcontent.com/pod-product-compliance
Lightning Source LLC
Chambersburg PA
CBHW032027040426
42448CB00006B/746